# Florida's Fight for Equality

Kelly Rodgers

## Consultants

**Dorothy Levin, M.S.Ed., MBA**
St. Lucie County Schools

**Vanessa Ann Gunther, Ph.D.**
Department of History
Chapman University

**Cassandra Slone**
Pinellas County Public Schools

## Publishing Credits

Rachelle Cracchiolo, M.S.Ed., *Publisher*
Conni Medina, M.A.Ed., *Managing Editor*
Emily R. Smith, M.A.Ed., *Series Developer*
Diana Kenney, M.A.Ed., NBCT, *Content Director*
Courtney Patterson, *Multimedia Designer*

**Image Credits:** Cover and pp.1, 20, 21 (back and top) State Archives of Florida; pp.2-3 Everett Collection Historical/Alamy; p.4 LOC [LC-DIG-pga-03412]; p.5 (front) NARA [542069]; p.6 (bottom) Granger, NYC; pp.6 (top), 31 Internet Archive/Public Domain; p.7 LOC [LC-DIG-pga-04167]; pp.8-9 Library of Congress, Prints & Photographs Division, Visual Materials from the NAACP Records [LC-DIG-ppmsca-05523]; p.9 Sandra Baker/Alamy; pp.10 (back), 29 (middle) Yale Collection of American Literature, Beinecke Rare Book and Manuscript Library; p.11 Ebyabe/Wikimedia Commons; pp.12, 29 (bottom) Afro American Newspapers/Gado/Getty Images; p.13 (bottom) LOC [LC-DIG-highsm-12536], (top) Creative Commons File:White hall.jpg by Lvklock, used under CC BY-SA 4.0; pp.14-15 LOC [LC-DIG-ppmsca-13256]; p.14 U.S. Air Force; p.16 (bottom) LOC [LC-DIG-fsa-8a03228]; pp.16-17 Bettmann/CORBIS; p.17 (top) HANDOUT/The Washington Post via Getty Images; p.18 (left) Historic Florida/Alamy; pp.18-19 Bettmann/CORBIS; p.19 (top) State Archives of Florida/Kerce; p.22 (left and right) NARA [299891]; pp.22-23 Wikimedia Commons/Public Domain; pp.24-25, 24 (bottom), 32 State Archives of Florida/Dughi; p.25 (bottom) Creative Commons Maurice Ferre by mauriceferre, used under CC BY 2.0; p.29 (top) Everett Collection Inc/Alamy; all other images from iStock and/or Shutterstock.

### Library of Congress Cataloging-in-Publication Data

Names: Rodgers, Kelly, author.
Title: Florida's fight for equality / Kelly Rodgers.
Description: Huntington Beach, CA : Teacher Created Materials, [2017] | Includes index.
Identifiers: LCCN 2016014358 (print) | LCCN 2016015184 (ebook) | ISBN 9781493835447 (pbk.) | ISBN 9781480756915 (eBook)
Subjects: LCSH: African Americans--Civil rights--Florida--History--20th century--Juvenile literature. | African Americans--Civil rights--Florida--History--19th century--Juvenile literature.
Classification: LCC F311.3 .R63 2017 (print) | LCC F311.3 (ebook) | DDC 323.1196/0730759--dc23
LC record available at https://lccn.loc.gov/2016014358

### Teacher Created Materials

5301 Oceanus Drive
Huntington Beach, CA 92649-1030
http://www.tcmpub.com

**ISBN 978-1-4938-3544-7**

© 2017 Teacher Created Materials, Inc.
Made in China
Nordica.082016.CA21601381

# Table of Contents

The Idea of Equality . . . . . . . . . . . . . . . . . . . . . . . 4
Early Leaders . . . . . . . . . . . . . . . . . . . . . . . . . . . . . 6
Fighting on Two Fronts. . . . . . . . . . . . . . . . . . . 14
The Fight Continues . . . . . . . . . . . . . . . . . . . . . 16
New Laws Change Lives. . . . . . . . . . . . . . . . . . 22
Human Rights Today . . . . . . . . . . . . . . . . . . . . 26
Analyze It! . . . . . . . . . . . . . . . . . . . . . . . . . . . . . 28
Glossary . . . . . . . . . . . . . . . . . . . . . . . . . . . . . . 30
Index . . . . . . . . . . . . . . . . . . . . . . . . . . . . . . . . . 31
Your Turn! . . . . . . . . . . . . . . . . . . . . . . . . . . . . . 32

# The Idea of Equality

Thomas Jefferson wrote the Declaration of Independence in 1776. He told of his dreams for the new country. He wrote, "We hold these truths to be self-evident, that all men are created equal."

Abraham Lincoln echoed that **decree** in 1861. He wrote that "liberty to all" was the key value that would give people hope. He called it America's "apple of gold." He said the U.S. Constitution should protect that freedom.

Freedoms that all people should have are called *civil rights*. Civil rights protect us from being treated unfairly. Yet, unfair laws took away the rights of many Americans even after Jefferson and Lincoln had penned their words.

People fought for civil rights for many years. They rallied. They protested. They joined together to have a stronger voice. These people aren't contained in one state. People from many states have done their part. They left their mark on history with their efforts.

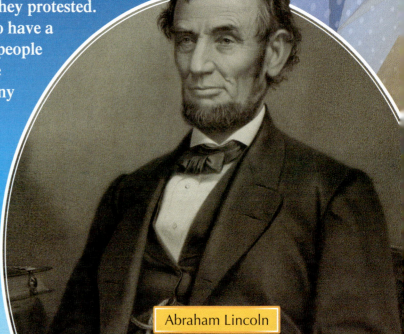

Abraham Lincoln

## Martin Luther King Jr.

Martin Luther King Jr. repeated the famous words from the Declaration of Independence in his "I Have A Dream" speech. He proclaimed, "I have a dream that one day this nation will rise up and live out the true meaning of its creed: 'We hold these truths to be self-evident, that all men are created equal.'"

# Early Leaders

One person who fought for civil rights was Timothy Thomas Fortune. Fortune was born into slavery in Florida in 1856. Even after his life as a slave came to an end, he witnessed much racial violence. Groups, such as the Ku Klux Klan, filled people with fear. He didn't want people to live like that.

Timothy Thomas Fortune

### Dangerous Enemies

Civil rights **activists** had dangerous enemies. One group was the Ku Klux Klan, or KKK. Members of this group terrorized African Americans. They threatened them. They kidnapped and tortured them. Many times, they killed them.

1874 political cartoon

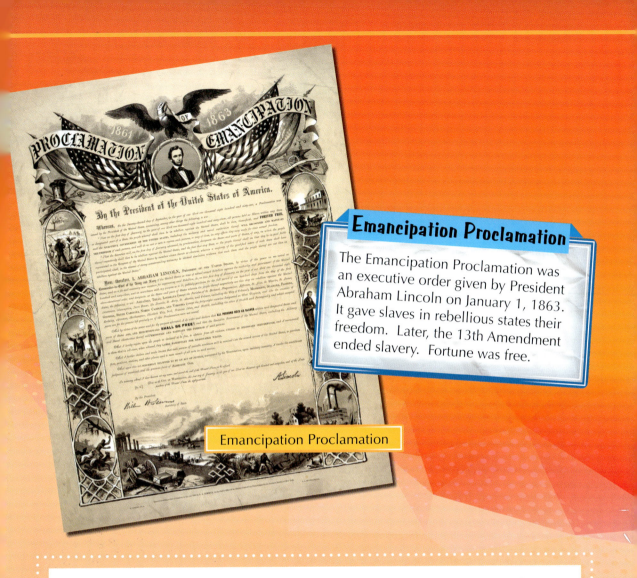

### Emancipation Proclamation

The Emancipation Proclamation was an executive order given by President Abraham Lincoln on January 1, 1863. It gave slaves in rebellious states their freedom. Later, the 13th Amendment ended slavery. Fortune was free.

Emancipation Proclamation

Fortune became a writer after a short bout in college. He wrote for a newspaper in 1876. It was called the *People's Advocate*. Soon, he married and had a child. He started his own newspaper called *The New York Globe* in 1881. He turned it into one of the leading black papers of the time. Although the paper changed names twice, it was his stage for writing about living conditions in the South. He asked for **equality**. He asked for integration.

Fortune did more to help in 1887 when he founded the Afro-American League. The members of this group fought at the state and local levels for voting and civil rights. They fought for education. They fought to end violence against African Americans.

## Founding the NAACP

The Afro-American League paved the way for groups such as the National Association for the Advancement of Colored People (NAACP). The NAACP was founded in 1909. It was formed in part because of the gruesome **lynchings** that took place at that time. Its goal was to guard the rights of all people regardless of race. But the group wanted to meet its goals peacefully. It wanted to **abide** by the law.

NAACP today

The NAACP had more than 90,000 members by 1919. They focused their efforts on getting support for new laws. They researched lynchings and **published** their findings. They investigated crimes. They protested injustice. They worked to evoke change.

The NAACP is still around. It continues to rely on its members to fight for equality. These men and women—young and old, rich and poor—have a shared passion regardless of their skin tone.

James Weldon Johnson

## The Power of Art

Another early leader was James Weldon Johnson. Johnson was born in Jacksonville, Florida, in 1871. Johnson's interests took him down many paths. He was a lawyer and a school principal in the late 1800s. He got into politics in the early 1900s. He joined the NAACP in 1916. For over 10 years, he was a voice against **racism** for the group.

But what really defined Johnson was his work as a writer. He held the firm belief that people could prove their worth through writing and art. He showed this in his own work.

Johnson wrote poetry, songs, and novels. One of his songs is called "Lift Every Voice and Sing." He wrote it with his brother for a school performance in honor of Lincoln's birthday. Students sang the song and shared it with others in the South. Its fame grew. The NAACP used the song as the "National Negro Anthem." It became an anthem for people fighting injustice.

### Stanton School

Johnson's song was written for and performed by students at Stanton School. Stanton was the first school created for black children in Florida. It was created during **Reconstruction** by the Freedman's Bureau (BYOOR-oh).

Mary McLeod Bethune

## Teaching Social Change

Johnson wasn't alone in his fight. Mary McLeod Bethune was born in South Carolina in 1875. Her parents had been slaves. But, she was born free. She moved to Florida after she got married. She became a teacher and a civil rights leader.

Bethune wanted to give poor black girls a place to get an education. She opened a school in Daytona in 1904. Only five girls went to the school when it opened. They had to pay 50 cents a week to attend. But the number of girls soon swelled to 250!

Bethune's goal was social change. She taught people to speak up for their rights. She led many groups that shared her goal. She was president of the Florida Federation of Colored Women for seven years. She went on to found the National Council for Negro Women in 1935. She even served as vice president of the NAACP from 1940 to 1955.

Bethune-Cookman University

### Status Change

Bethune's school became a college when it joined with another school in 1923. It came to be known as Bethune-Cookman College in 1931. Then, Bethune-Cookman College became Bethune-Cookman University in 2007.

# Fighting on Two Fronts

The United States joined World War II in 1941. More than 50,000 African Americans from Florida joined the armed forces. These black soldiers found themselves fighting two "wars." One was on the battlefield. The other was on the home front. They called this fight the Double V **campaign**. They fought for two "Vs," or victories. One was for the war. The other was for equal rights.

Daniel "Chappie" James was one of the black soldiers. James grew up in Florida. He went to school at the Tuskegee Institute in Alabama in 1937. He became one of the famed Tuskegee Airmen. These men were the first black pilots in the armed forces.

On several occasions, black officers went to a whites-only officers club. They were arrested. James was one of those men. James worked with people to get the charges dropped. One of those people was future Supreme Court Justice Thurgood Marshall. The charges were finally dropped. James was the only pilot who could fly a certain plane, so the army wanted him to keep flying.

### Daniel "Chappie" James

James also fought in the Korean and Vietnam wars. In 1975, he became the highest-ranking African American officer, a four-star general, in the U.S. Air Force.

Daniel "Chappie" James

Tuskegee Airmen

# The Fight Continues

Brave men and women continued to fight for equality. They fought for equal education. They fought for the right to vote. They fought for their rights as **citizens**.

The civil rights movement got some help from the Supreme Court in 1954. That help came from a court case known as *Brown v. Board of Education of Topeka, Kansas*. In this landmark case, the court ruled that separate schools for black and white students broke the law. They said separate was not equal. The decision was a huge victory.

Still, change was slow to come to Florida. Many fought against the changes. They did not accept that people needed to be treated the same way in schools. But the change sparked more action. Many people protested and made their voices heard. They wanted **segregation** in schools to end in the state. But school was not the only place people wanted to be equal.

## Harry T. and Harriette Moore

Harry T. and Harriette Moore were a husband and wife team who set up new chapters of the NAACP in Florida in 1934. In 1937, they filed a lawsuit to help black teachers get equal pay. On Christmas Day in 1951, Harry was killed by a bomb blast at their home. Harriette died nine days later from her injuries.

Thurgood Marshall

Thurgood Marshall stands with fellow attorneys after winning *Brown v. Board of Education of Topeka, Kansas.*

Wilhelmina Jakes and Carrie Patterson were Florida A&M students in 1956. In May of that year, they sat in the whites-only part of a Tallahassee city bus. They would not move to the back of the bus. They said it was too full. They offered to leave the bus if they got their fares back. The driver said no. They were arrested. This started the Tallahassee Bus **Boycott**. African Americans around the city stopped riding buses. They asked others not to ride, too. The actions of a few caught the eyes of many.

But there was another case brewing that helped the people of Tallahassee. The Supreme Court ruled in December that segregation on buses was against the law. People in Florida wanted to know if this ruling would be upheld in their state. Members of a group called the Inter-Civic Council (ICC) tried it out. They rode the buses. They were not asked to move to the back of the bus! By 1958, segregation on Florida's city buses ended.

Reverend C.K. Steele (middle) walks into a courthouse.

### Strong as Steele

Many black church leaders were active in the civil rights movement. Reverend C.K. Steele was one such leader. He helped organize the ICC. He also organized a carpool system to help people get around during the boycott.

### LeRoy Collins

LeRoy Collins became governor of Florida in 1955. As governor, Collins was known to support civil rights. However, in response to the bus boycott, he said the ICC was "pushing too hard, too fast."

Black students wave at an empty bus during the Tallahassee Bus Boycott.

**Sit-ins** were also held as protests during this time. On February 20, 1960, 17 Florida A&M and Florida State University students went to a Woolworth lunch counter in Tallahassee. When they would not leave, 11 of them were arrested. The students were given a choice. They could pay a 300-dollar fine or serve 60 days in jail. All but 3 chose jail time. These 8 students held the first "jail-in" and served 49 days.

Protests also reached Florida's beaches as early as 1945 and continued through the 1960s. Lawson Thomas and Ira P. Davis started "wade-ins." They asked black beachgoers to go to beaches and get in the water. It turns out that there were no laws against black swimmers at the beach. Even so, wade-ins started taking place all over the state. Black swimmers stayed peaceful. But their white opponents did not. White beachgoers and groups like the KKK often attacked the swimmers.

wade-in at a Fort Lauderdale beach

Three students appear in court after being charged with unlawful assembly at the March 13, 1960 sit-in.

Students participate in a sit-in on March 13, 1960, despite the February 20 arrests.

# New Laws Change Lives

The fight for civil rights continued in Florida and other states. President John F. Kennedy asked the nation to stay calm. He said it was time for change. He asked Congress to pass a new law. He sent a civil rights bill to Congress that would give all people in the country equal rights. It was called the Civil Rights Act. It would ban segregation. It would guard the rights of all people. In the bill, he wrote "the nation…will not be free until all its citizens are free." Sadly, Kennedy was killed in 1963 before the law passed.

President Lyndon B. Johnson took up the fight. He thought the new law was important. He got Congress to pass the Civil Rights Act of 1964. He helped make other changes, too. Congress passed the Voting Rights Act in 1965. This law protected the rights of black voters. Laws began to change. Racist practices began to change. But they did not end.

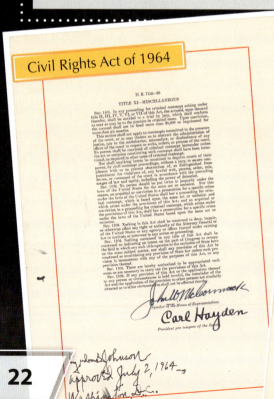

Civil Rights Act of 1964

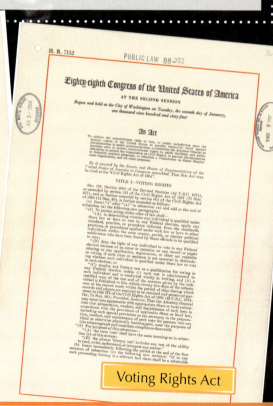

Voting Rights Act

### A Visit to St. Augustine

Martin Luther King Jr. went to St. Augustine in spring of 1964. He wanted to garner support for the Civil Rights Act that had not yet passed. He launched a local campaign to bring equality to the country's oldest city.

Martin Luther King Jr.

President Lyndon B. Johnson signs the Civil Rights Act of 1964.

Gwen Cherry

Gwen Cherry

New laws said that separate was not equal. But racism was still rampant. African Americans were not the only group to face this problem.

Women of all races joined the fight for civil rights, too. Gwendolyn "Gwen" Cherry was one such person. She was born in Miami in 1923. She became a teacher when she grew up. Then, she went to law school. She was the first black female law student at the University of Miami. She was also the first black female lawyer in Dade County. Cherry was elected to Florida's House of Representatives in 1970. She believed that women needed laws to protect them. She wanted to help pass those laws.

Maurice Ferré also made his mark on the state. Ferré was a strong voice for Hispanics while he served in the House of Representatives from 1967 to 1968. He was also the first Puerto Rican-born mayor of any U.S. city. He has stayed active in public service since his time in office.

Maurice Ferré

# Human Rights Today

The end of slavery did not result in fairness for all. When one struggle ended, a new one began. People were not viewed as equal. They did not have the same rights. African Americans fought for civil rights. They fought against unfair laws. Brave men and women—black and white—led the way.

These people laid the groundwork for equality. Sit-ins, boycotts, and rallies brought them into the news. People risked their safety and their lives to drive change.

Efforts continue today. New civil rights groups have joined the fight for equal treatment. The National Organization for Women is among those groups. So is the Human Rights Campaign. People whose voices were once muted are now speaking out. They are making it clear that America's "apple of gold" should be everyone's for the taking.

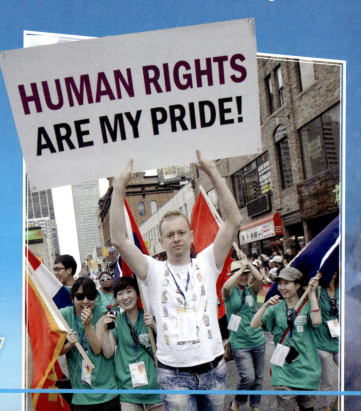

# Analyze It!

James Weldon Johnson wanted to help African Americans overcome racism and segregation. He and his brother wrote a song that told of unity, hope, and perseverance. Soon, the song became the anthem of the civil rights movement.

Read the song lyrics below. Analyze the words Johnson used to signify unity, hope, and perseverance. Then, write your own song lyrics that support the work of the civil rights movement.

## Lift Every Voice and Sing

*By James Weldon Johnson*

Lift every voice and sing,

Till earth and heaven ring,

Ring with the harmonies of Liberty;

Let our rejoicing rise

High as the list'ning skies,

Let it resound loud as the rolling sea.

Sing a song full of the faith that the dark past has taught us,

Sing a song full of the hope that the present has brought us;

Facing the rising sun of our new day begun,

Let us march on till victory is won.

# Glossary

**abide**—to accept something

**activists**—people who use or support strong actions, such as protests, to make changes

**boycott**—to not buy, use, or participate in something as a way to protest

**campaign**—a series of organized activities designed to achieve a particular result

**citizens**—people who live in a country and have rights of that country

**decree**—an official order given by a person in power

**equality**—being treated in the same way and having the same rights

**lynchings**—a hate crime in which people who do not abide by a narrow code of conduct are brutally murdered

**published**—made information known to the public

**racism**—the belief that some races of people are superior over others

**Reconstruction**—the years after the Civil War when the country reformed

**segregation**—the practice of separating groups of people based on their race or religion

**sit-ins**—protests in which groups of people sit or stay in a place and refuse to leave

# Index

Bethune, Mary McLeod, 12–13

*Brown v. Board of Education of Topeka, Kansas*, 16–17

Cherry, Gwendolyn "Gwen," 24

Civil Rights Act of 1964, 22–23

Collins, LeRoy, 19

Declaration of Independence, 4–5

Double V campaign, 14

Ferré, Maurice, 25

Fortune, Timothy Thomas, 6–7

Jakes, Wilhelmina, 18

James, Daniel "Chappie," 14

Johnson, James Weldon, 10–12, 28

Johnson, Lyndon B., 22–23

Kennedy, John F., 22

Ku Klux Klan, 6

"Lift Every Voice and Sing," 11, 28

Moore, Harriette, 17

Moore, Harry T., 17

NAACP (National Association for the Advancement of Colored People), 8–9, 11–12, 17

Patterson, Carrie, 18

Stanton School, 11

Steele, C.K., 18

Tallahassee Bus Boycott, 18–19

U.S. Constitution, 4

Voting Rights Act, 22

# Your Turn!

## Freedom of Speech

The right to freedom of speech is something that every United States citizen is entitled to. What do you feel passionately about? Why do you think it's important? What would happen if we no longer had that right? Write a speech that tells about your cause.